Pebble® Plus

THE U.S. MILITARY BRANCHES
THE U.S. ARMY

by Matt Doeden

CAPSTONE PRESS
a capstone imprint

TF WINGS
E-FRS
LOADTEST DUE
7/13
N/I 06 / 08
7.00
207706
WARNING
CAUTION
WARNING
WARNING
WARNING
CAUTION
24 VOLTS DC

The Army has many
other jobs. Some soldiers
are doctors or cooks.
Others build bridges
or play music.

Glossary

Armed Forces—the whole military; the U.S. Armed Forces include the Army, Navy, Air Force, Marine Corps, and Coast Guard

armor—a protective metal covering

branch—a part of a larger group

grenade—a small bomb that can be thrown or launched

infantry—a group of people in the military trained to fight on land

mechanic—a person who fixes machines

missile—an explosive weapon that is thrown or shot at a distant target

rifle—a long-barreled gun that is fired from the shoulder

tank—an armored vehicle that moves on two tracks

target—an object at which to aim or shoot

Read More

Callery, Sean. *Branches of the Military*. Discover More Readers. New York: Scholastic, 2015.

Marx, Mandy R. *Amazing U.S. Army Facts*. Amazing Military Facts. North Mankato, Minn.: Capstone Press, 2017.

Murray, Julie. *United States Army*. U.S. Armed Forces. Minneapolis: Abdo Kids, 2015.

Internet Sites

FactHound offers a safe, fun way to find Internet sites related to this book. All of the sites on FactHound have been researched by our staff.

Here's all you do:
Visit *www.facthound.com*
Type in this code: 9781515767732

Check out projects, games and lots more at
www.capstonekids.com